Habitats

All About
Oceans

raintree

a Capstone company — publishers for children

Raintree is an imprint of Capstone Global Library Limited, a company incorporated in England and Wales having its registered office at 264 Banbury Road, Oxford, OX2 7DY – Registered company number: 6695582

www.raintree.co.uk
myorders@raintree.co.uk

Edited by Kristen Mohn
Designed by Juliette Peters
Picture research by Wanda Winch
Production by Steve Walker
Originated by Capstone Global Library Limited
Printed and bound in China

ISBN 978-1-4747-4724-0
21 20 19 18 17
10 9 8 7 6 5 4 3 2 1

British Library Cataloguing-in-Publication Data
A full catalogue record for this book is available from the British Library

Acknowledgements
We would like to thank the following for permission to reproduce photographs: Minden Pictures: Hiroya Minakuchi, 17; Shutterstock: Bokasana, starfish design, wave design, CO Leong, 19, David Litman, 15, Kajonsak Tui, 9, KGrif, 13, Kjeld Friis, 7, mashe, 11, Soren Egeberg Photography, 21, Tanya Puntti, 5, Willyam Bradberry, cover, 1

Every effort has been made to contact copyright holders of material reproduced in this book. Any omissions will be rectified in subsequent printings if notice is given to the publisher.

All the internet addresses (URLs) given in this book were valid at the time of going to press. However, due to the dynamic nature of the internet, some addresses may have changed, or sites may have changed or ceased to exist since publication. While the author and publisher regret any inconvenience this may cause readers, no responsibility for any such changes can be accepted by either the author or the publisher.

Contents

What is an ocean?

An ocean is a big body of salt water. Plants and animals live in oceans.

Their homes are called habitats.

Most homes are in water.

Some are on shore.

The shore

Waves roll in.

Crabs hide in the sand.

Birds hunt.

ghost crab

Waves roll out.

Starfish hold

on to rocks.

The open ocean

The sun warms the open ocean.

Kelp grows.

Fish live in the kelp.

kelp

Seals eat the fish.

Sharks hunt.

leopard shark

The deep sea

The deep sea is cold
and dark.

Big whales dive here.

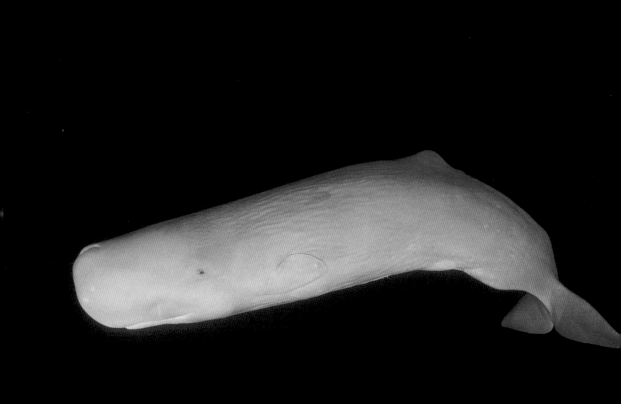

sperm whale

It is hard to see in the dark.

Some animals grow big eyes.

Others glow!

jellyfish

The waves roll in and out.

Life is on the move in the ocean.

Glossary

crab   sea animal with a wide, flat shell and two front claws

deep sea   bottom of the ocean where it is cold and dark

habitat   home of a plant or animal

kelp   big, brown plant that grows in the ocean

open ocean   top of the ocean, far from land

shore   part of the ocean where the water ends and the land begins

starfish   sea animal that has five arms and is shaped like a star

Read more

i-SPY at the Seaside: What can You Spot? (Collins Michelin i-SPY Guides), i-SPY (Collins, 2016)

Little Kids First Big Book of the Ocean (National Geographic Little Kids), Katherine D Hughes (National Geographic Kids, 2013)

Oceans (Eyewonder), DK (DK Children, 2015)

Websites

www.bbc.co.uk/education/clips/zx676sg

www.ducksters.com/geography/oceans.php

www.theschoolrun.com/homework-help/coastal-habitats

Index